Early TOY Encyclopedias

HOT WHEELS

by A. W. Buckey

Early Encyclopedias

An Imprint of Abdo Reference
abdobooks.com

abdobooks.com

Published by Abdo Reference, a division of ABDO, PO Box 398166, Minneapolis, Minnesota 55439.

Printed in China.
052025
092025

Editor: Christa Kelly
Series Designers: Candice Keimig, Joshua Olson
Production Designer: Ryan Gale

Library of Congress Control Number: 2024949189

Publisher's Cataloging-in-Publication Data

Names: Buckey, A. W., author.
Title: Hot Wheels / by A. W. Buckey
Description: Minneapolis, Minnesota: Abdo Reference, 2026 | Series: Early toy encyclopedias | Includes online resources and index.
Identifiers: ISBN 9781098297558 (lib. bdg.) | ISBN 9798384930075 (ebook)
Subjects: LCSH: Hot Wheels toys--Juvenile literature. | Toy automobiles--Juvenile literature. | Toys--Juvenile literature. | Collectibles--Juvenile literature. | Reference materials--Juvenile literature. | Encyclopedias and dictionaries--Juvenile literature.
Classification: DDC 688.6--dc23

CONTENTS

Hot Wheels

Hot Wheels are toy vehicles. Most are cars. They are made by a toy company called Mattel. Hot Wheels are known for being fast and detailed.

Hot Rods

The first Hot Wheels car was made in the 1960s in Los Angeles, California. At the time, cars known as hot rods were popular. These were cars that drivers changed to be faster. People gave their cars new engines.

FUN FACT!

Elliot Handler was a cofounder of Mattel. He helped create Hot Wheels.

Some hot rods are built for racing. Others are built to be shown off.

Hot Wheels is the most popular toy car brand in the world.

They painted the cars in flashy colors. Mattel wanted to make hot rod toys. The company hired a car designer to help.

Designing and Building

Mattel designed the toy cars in 1:64 scale. This meant that the cars were about 64 times smaller than real cars. Workers then made the cars out of metal. Finally, the cars were painted with shiny Spectraflame paint.

Spectraflame

Hot Wheels originally came in 12 different Spectraflame colors.

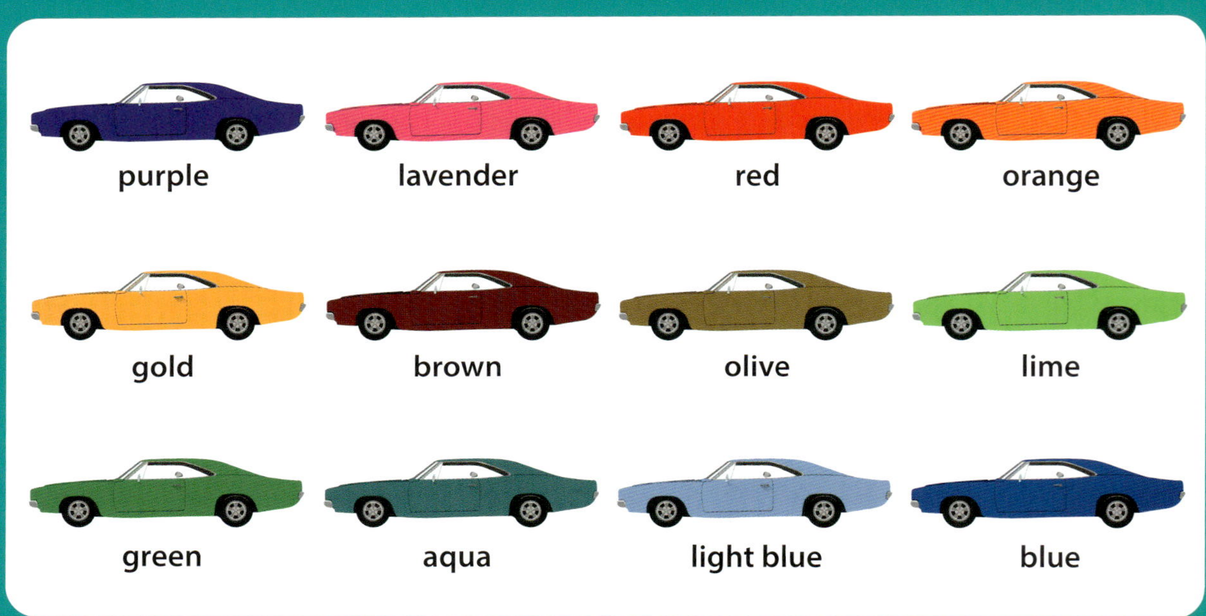

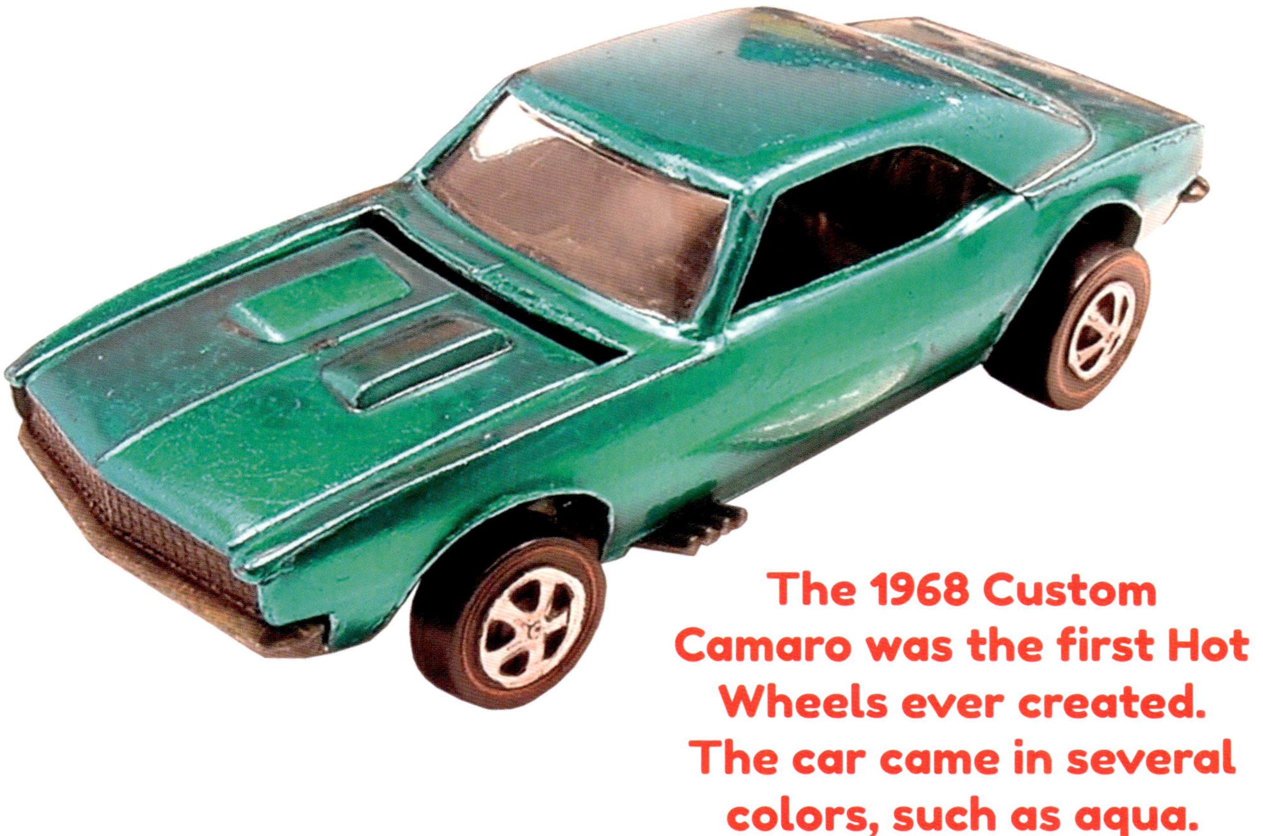

The 1968 Custom Camaro was the first Hot Wheels ever created. The car came in several colors, such as aqua.

The First Hot Wheels

The first 16 Hot Wheels were released in 1968. They were all based on real cars. They became known as the Sweet 16. A new brand was born.

After Spectraflame

Spectraflame paint was made with a dangerous ingredient called lead. In 1973, the paint was banned. Designers replaced Spectraflame with other types of paint.

Spectraflame paint made the Sweet 16 eye catching and exciting.

Competition

In 1968, Mattel showed the Sweet 16 at the International Toy Fair. Then the company sent the toy cars to stores. Hot Wheels were not the first toy cars on the market. Brands such as Matchbox and Corgi made similar toys. But commercials said Hot Wheels were "the fastest metal cars you've ever seen!"

Hot Wheels Tires

The first Hot Wheels cars had hard plastic tires. These tires rolled easily and quickly over surfaces.

Selling Hot Wheels

The first Hot Wheels cost up to $0.89 each. That's about eight dollars in today's money. The company promoted the toys by giving them out for free at gas stations. Hot Wheels quickly became very popular.

Hot Wheels were advertised in comic books and on TV.

New from Mattel. Action sets for the fastest miniature metal cars you've ever seen!

New Hot Wheels out-race, out-stunt, out-distance any other kind of miniature car.

Hot Wheels Logo

Mattel advertises Hot Wheels with a famous flame design. The flame represents the speed and excitement of Hot Wheels cars. In the 1970s, Hot Wheels introduced a slogan. It was "Go with the winner."

The Hot Wheels logo has changed over the brand's history.

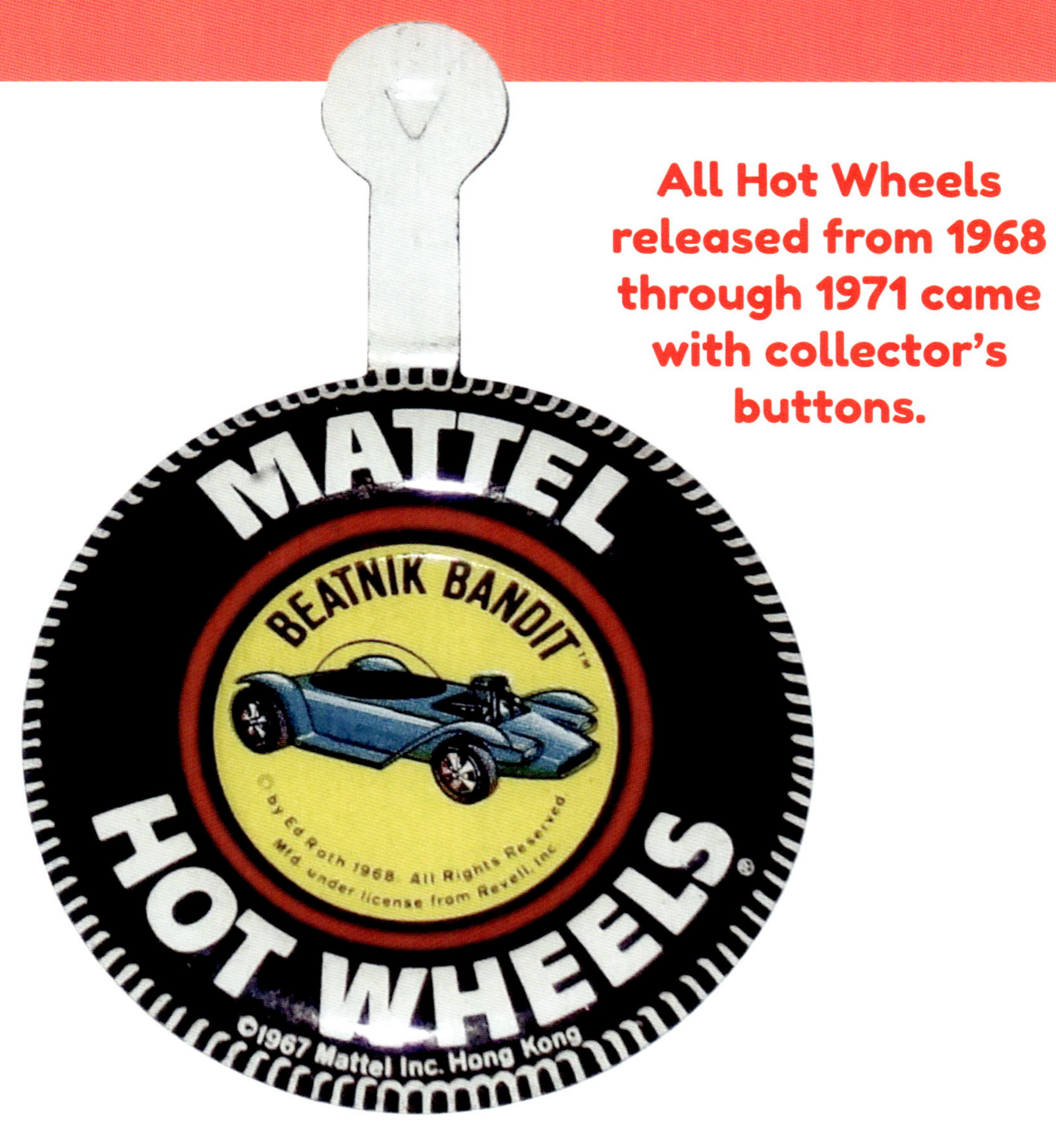

All Hot Wheels released from 1968 through 1971 came with collector's buttons.

Collector's Buttons

Early Hot Wheels came with collector's buttons. These buttons were made of plastic or metal. They had a picture of a Hot Wheels car on the front.

There are more Hot Wheels on earth than real cars.

Hot Wheels Today

Today, Hot Wheels are the best-selling toys in the world. There are more than 20,000 different kinds of Hot Wheels. The brand also makes construction vehicles, motorcycles, and airplanes. Some cost less than two dollars. Others are so rare that collectors pay thousands of dollars for them.

A Lifelong Hobby

The Hot Wheels brand has expanded to include books, movies, TV shows, and video games. There are real-life Hot Wheels events. Amusement parks have Hot Wheels–themed rides. And Hot Wheels fans meet to race and show off their collections. Collecting and racing Hot Wheels can be a lifelong hobby.

People of all ages can play with and collect Hot Wheels.

Hot Wheels Manufacturing

Hot Wheels cars are made in several locations in Asia. The biggest Hot Wheels plant is in Malaysia. Malaysia is a country in Southeast Asia. Its factories produce many goods, such as electronics.

Malaysia's biggest Hot Wheels manufacturing plant is in Penang.

China, Peru, and Australia produce more than half the world's zinc.

Materials

Metal Hot Wheels are made from a zinc-based alloy. The alloy also contains aluminum. These metals are mined from under the ground.

Die casting was invented in 1838.

Die Casting

Hot Wheels come in many shapes and sizes. But most are made in similar ways. Designers create a mold. Then metal is melted. It is poured into the mold. This process is called die casting.

Down the Conveyor Belt

The metal parts cool. Then they drop onto a conveyor belt. Workers separate the car parts from any scraps. The scraps are melted down to be reused. Car parts that will be painted are hung on poles. They are then sprayed with paint.

Parts of a Hot Wheels

Most Hot Wheels cars have similar parts.

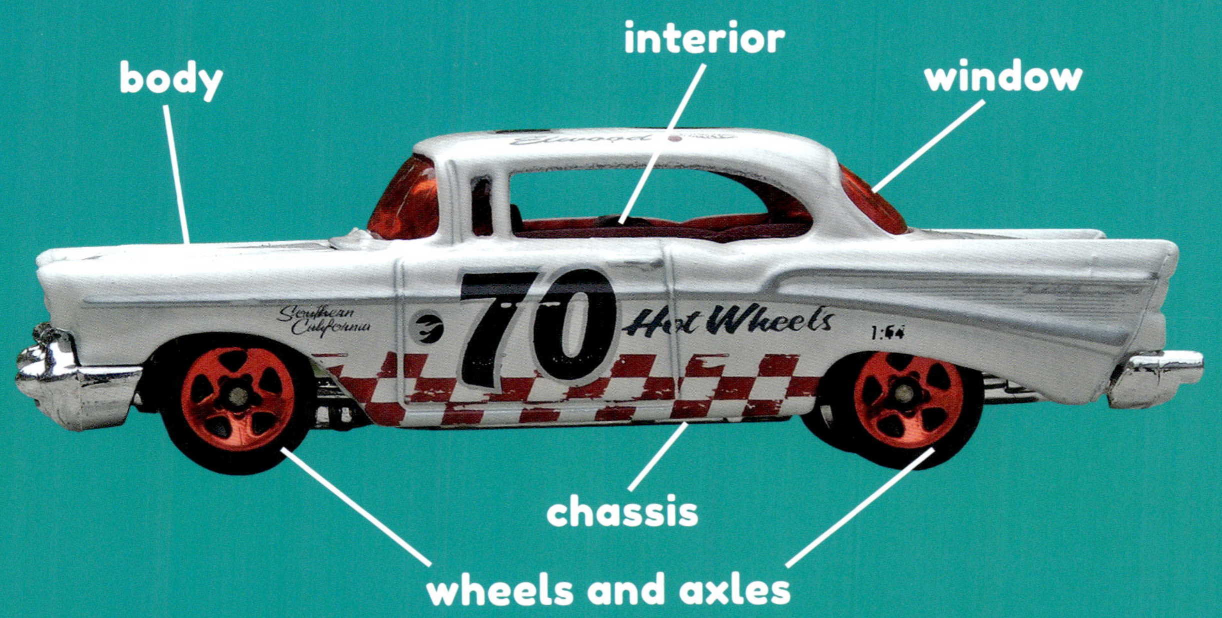

Tampo Printing

Parts that need graphics are placed on a conveyor belt for tampo printing. Tampo printing is an easy way to get detailed graphics on objects. Paint is pressed onto rubber pads. The pads are then pressed onto the vehicles. The paint transfers from the pads to the vehicles.

FUN FACT!

More than six billion Hot Wheels cars have been made.

Hot Wheels started using tampo printing in 1974.

About 16 Hot Wheels are made each second.

Assembly

The parts are finally put together. A machine presses on the pieces to secure them. Once the car is finished, it is put in packaging. It is ready to be sold.

The Custom Police Cruiser came out in 1969. In 1970, a new version came out painted like a fire truck.

The Grand Prix

After the Sweet 16, Hot Wheels designers made a new set of cars. This set included a police car called the Custom Police Cruiser. In 1969, Hot Wheels introduced another set called the Grand Prix. This was a set of eight racing cars.

Twin Mill

The Twin Mill was the first Hot Wheels that was not based on a real car. It has a bullet-shaped body and two large engines. It has no doors. The top instead opens upward to give access to the interior. The Twin Mill was later made into a real full-size car.

Custom Police Cruiser

The Custom Police Cruiser has a siren on its roof and a painted sheriff's badge on its side. The car was designed by Ira Gilford.

Many people consider the Twin Mill to be Hot Wheels' most iconic car.

Tri Baby

In 1970, Hot Wheels released the Tri Baby. It was designed to look like a futuristic sports car. It has a long, sleek body. The back can be lifted up to expose the engine.

Since its release, several new versions of the Tri Baby have been sold.

The Side Kick was designed by Larry Wood.

Side Kick

Hot Wheels designers added special features to some of their cars. The 1972 Side Kick has exhaust pipes with a hidden trick. People can pull on the pipes to make the driver's seat slide out.

Snake's real name is Don Prudhomme.

Snake and Mongoose

In 1970, Hot Wheels sponsored two drag racers. Drag racers compete in car races. The drivers of the cars were nicknamed Snake and Mongoose. Mattel sold cars based on Snake's and Mongoose's race cars.

The 1970 Mongoose

Mongoose drove a Plymouth Duster funny car. Funny cars are drag racing cars. The outside part of a funny car can detach from the base and be lifted up and down. The body of the 1970 Mongoose Hot Wheels car can be detached just like on a real funny car.

FUN FACT!

Though Snake and Mongoose raced against each other, they were close friends.

Tom McEwen, better known as Mongoose, raced for 45 years.

Redline Era

From 1968 to 1977, most Hot Wheels cars had a red stripe along the side of their wheels. This period is known as the Redline Era of Hot Wheels. Hot Wheels with these stripes are known as Redlines.

The Redline wheels were designed by Howard Newman.

The black wheels used on newer cars are known as basic wheels.

End of an Era

In 1977, Mattel decided to remove the red line from its tires. The line had gone out of style on real cars. The company wanted its vehicles to look like the popular cars on the street. Removing the line also helped Mattel save money.

Many Hot Wheels tracks are a distinctive orange color.

Hot Wheels Tracks

The Hot Wheels brand eventually expanded beyond cars. Mattel built plastic racetracks to allow buyers to race their cars. Some had multiple levels. Many had special features such as loops or jumps.

The Super-Charger

In 1969, Hot Wheels released a track set called the Super-Charger. This track set has a fuel station. Inside the station are wheels powered by a motor. Cars speed up when they pass by the wheels. This allows cars to zoom around the track at high speeds.

The Super-Charger has several speed options.

Harry Bradley

Hot Wheels designers create unique designs for new toy cars. One of the first Hot Wheels designers was Harry Bradley. Bradley worked at the car company General Motors. He used his knowledge to make the first Hot Wheels.

Harry Bradley worked as a car designer at General Motors.

Bradley designed both the full-size Deora and the model Hot Wheels Deora.

The Deora

The Deora was one of Bradley's Sweet 16 designs. It was based on a show car from the car company Dodge. Show cars are created to display new, interesting designs. They are not made to be sold. The Deora has an unusual design. Passengers get inside by lifting the front windshield.

Suspension

Cars use suspension to smooth bumps and bounces from the road. The first Hot Wheels cars had suspension. This helped them roll smoothly.

Ira Gilford worked at Hot Wheels from 1967 to 1970. He designed the Spoilers in 1970.

Ira Gilford

Ira Gilford was Bradley's friend. Gilford had worked at the Chrysler car company. He designed the Twin Mill. He also helped create a line of Hot Wheels called Spoilers. These cars have engines on the outside of the bodies.

Splittin' Image

Splittin' Image is a Gilford design. It looks like two of the same car stuck together. It has two driver's seats. The car also has two exhaust pipes in the back. It is one of the most common early Hot Wheels cars.

Splittin' Image was released in 1969.

Larry Wood

In 1969, Larry Wood joined the Hot Wheels team. He stayed for more than 40 years. His first design was the Tri Baby. He went on to create hundreds of Hot Wheels designs. Wood was honored with a place in the Automotive Hall of Fame in 2023.

Larry Wood is often called Mr. Hot Wheels.

The Ramblin' Wrecker features Larry's name on the truck's side.

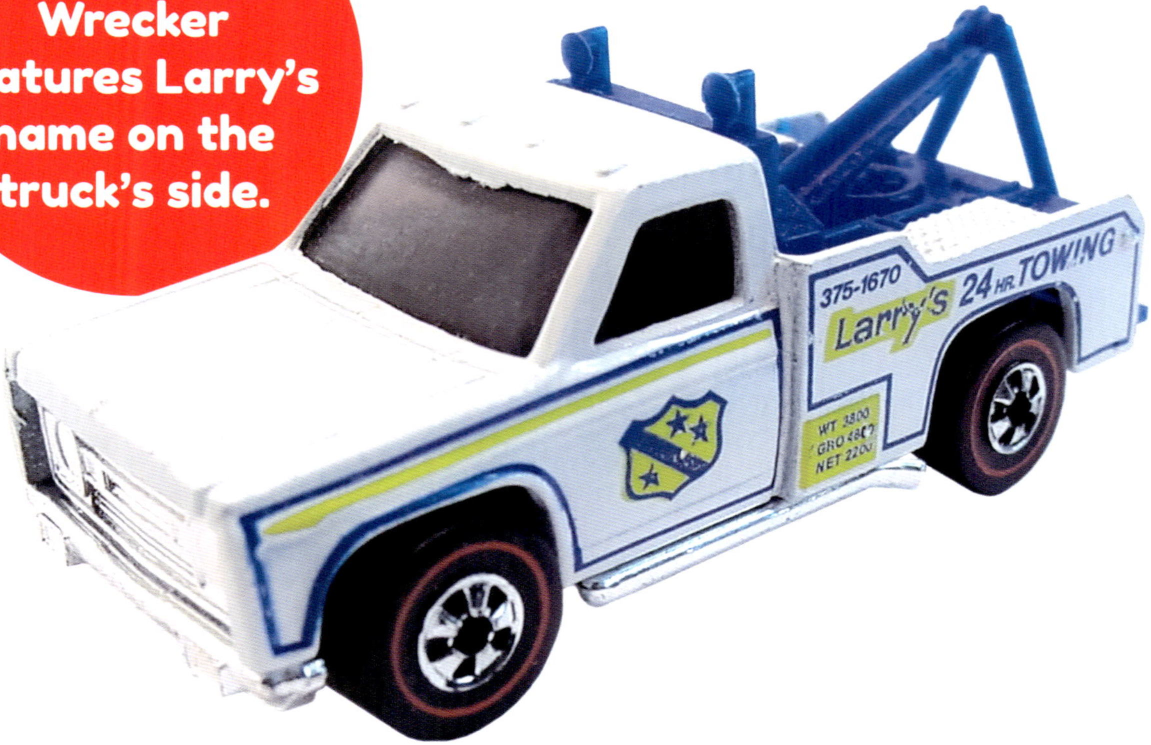

Ramblin' Wrecker

The Ramblin' Wrecker is a tow truck designed by Wood. It was released in 1975. A tow truck is a vehicle that moves cars. The Ramblin' Wrecker has a toy chain and hook to move cars.

The first Ramblin' Wrecker had Wood's phone number printed on the side. He got many calls.

Ryu Asada was born in Osaka, Japan.

Ryu Asada

Ryu Asada joined the Hot Wheels team in 2012. He became a lead designer. Asada passed away in 2021. The Ryu Asada Award was made in his honor. This award honors people who make creative car designs.

Duck N' Roll

Asada designed a toy car called the Duck N' Roll. This car is shaped like a rubber duck. The Duck N' Roll comes in a few different varieties. One version glows in the dark.

The Duck N' Roll was released in 2020.

Lindsey Lee

No women worked as full-time Hot Wheels designers until 2016. Lindsey Lee was the first. She worked on many Hot Wheels projects.

Lindsey Lee designed the Daisy Duck Hot Wheels.

RV There Yet

Lee created a design called the RV There Yet. It was part of the Tooned collection of Hot Wheels. These toys have soft lines and bubbly shapes to make them look like cartoon vehicles. The RV There Yet is a plastic car attached to a metal camper.

Sizzlers can reach a speed of 13.7 miles per hour (22 kmh).

Sizzlers

Hot Wheels released a line of cars called Sizzlers in 1970. These cars have electric motors and rechargeable batteries. The motors allow Sizzlers to complete bigger loops and longer tracks than traditional Hot Wheels.

Hot Wheels Convertables

In 1991, Hot Wheels released a line of cars called Convertables. These cars change color and shape in water. Some of the cars have roofs that collapse. These toys were not sold for very long.

At least 12 Convertables were planned for release, but only eight were ever sold.

Long Haulers

In 1998, Hot Wheels launched a line of semitrucks. Semitrucks carry goods across the country. Hot Wheels called the line Long Haulers. Each truck came with a car that it could carry. Since then, Hot Wheels has released many more semitrucks.

The Long Haulers were sold for only two years.

Unlike most Hot Wheels cars, the Robo Wheels robots are made of plastic.

Robo Wheels

In 2001, Hot Wheels introduced a new line called Robo Wheels. These cars can transform into robots. Along with text on the toys' packaging, a short movie and a series of commercials told the story of the robots.

The VW Bug was part of the 2005 Hot Wheels Mystery Cars series.

Hot Wheels Mystery Cars

Hot Wheels released a line of four Mystery Cars in 2005. The cars were hidden behind black plastic. Buyers could not tell which car they were getting. Each car came with a different voucher. The vouchers came together to make a picture of a Volkswagen Drag Bus. People who mailed all four vouchers to Hot Wheels received the bus as a prize.

Hot Wheels Color Shifters

Hot Wheels released new color-changing cars in 2008. They were called Color Shifters. These cars change color in hot water. Dipping the toys in ice-cold water changes them back.

FUN FACT!

Hot Wheels has released several lines of color-changing cars.

The original Color Shifters came in more than 30 designs.

Hot Wheels Mystery Models

In 2011, Hot Wheels released a line called Mystery Models. Like with the 2005 Mystery Cars, buyers could not tell which car they were purchasing. The cars came wrapped in dark foil.

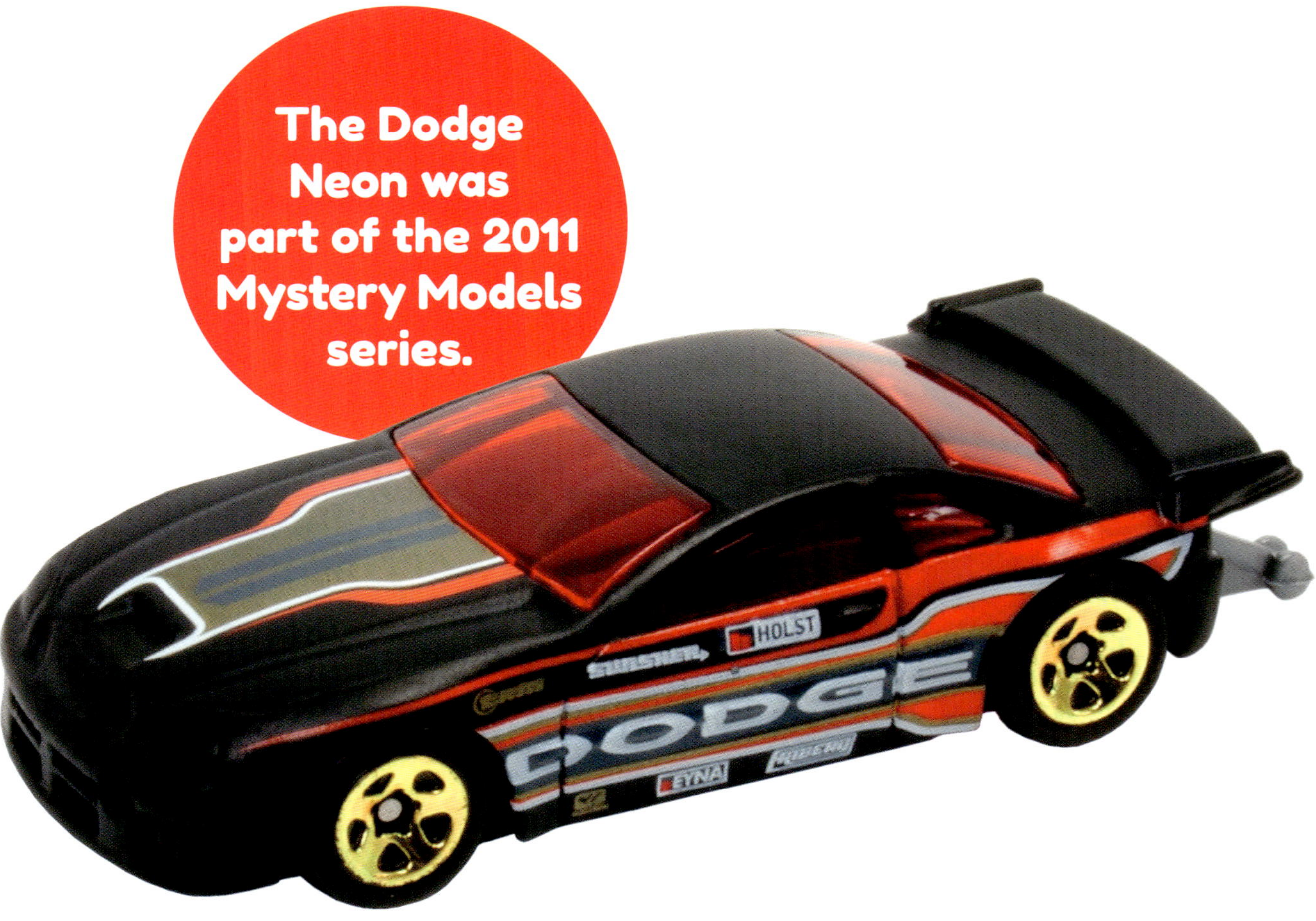

The Dodge Neon was part of the 2011 Mystery Models series.

Loopsters

A new line of cars called Loopsters was released in 2011. These cars look like roller-coaster cars. Each holds four tiny passengers. Connectors on the fronts and backs of the cars allow the Hot Wheels to connect to other Loopsters. This lets buyers make roller-coaster trains.

Experimotors

The 2017 Experimotors line allows people to tinker with their cars. Each Experimotors Hot Wheels has a special feature or moveable part. More Experimotors were released in the following years.

Monster Trucks

In 2018, Hot Wheels released a line of monster trucks. Monster trucks are giant, heavy trucks.

They have massive wheels and heavy suspensions. The suspensions help them make jumps and crush objects. In 2019, Hot Wheels released another line of monster trucks. This line included a model of Bigfoot, the first monster truck ever created.

FUN FACT!

Some Hot Wheels monster trucks glow in the dark.

Some Hot Wheels monster trucks come with cars to destroy.

True 1:64 Cars

Hot Wheels cars are usually in 1:64 scale. But this measurement is not always exact. Hot Wheels based on real cars are usually a little bigger or smaller than 1:64. However, there are a few Hot Wheels that are created in exactly 1:64 scale. The 2023 and 2024 Elite 64 series include ten true 1:64-sized cars.

The Audi RS 7 Sportback was part of the 2023 Elite 64 series.

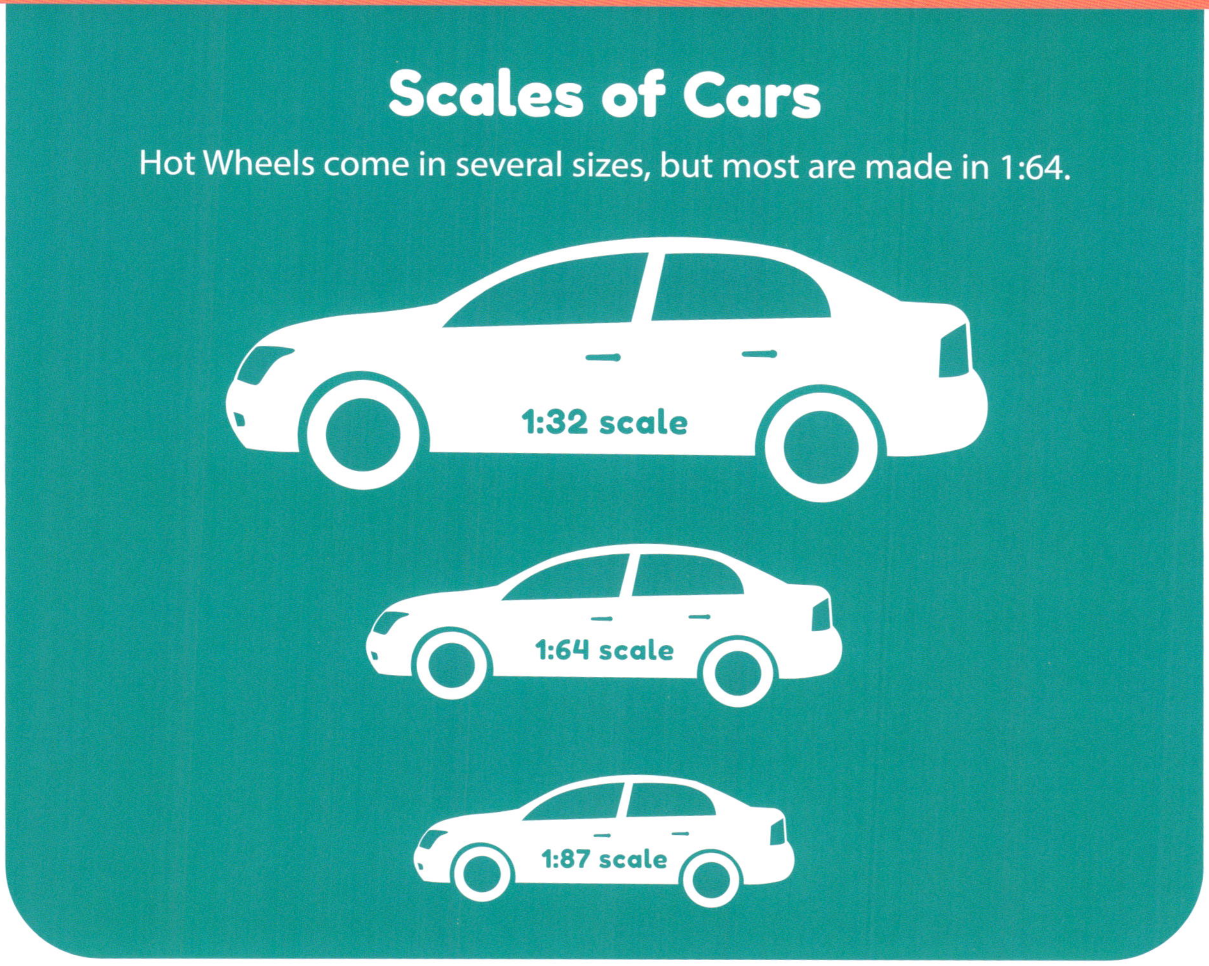

Other Scales

Some Hot Wheels come in larger or smaller sizes. The 2011 Cars of the Decade series was made in 1:32 scale. That is twice the size of an average Hot Wheels. The Atomix Hot Wheels is a series of extra-small Hot Wheels.

Marvel

Hot Wheels partners with other brands to make cars based on popular characters. These cars are called character cars. In the 1970s, Hot Wheels partnered with Marvel Comics. They worked together to make a line of cars called the Heroes. The Heroes features cars based on different superheroes, including Captain America, Iron Man, and Spider-Man.

Captain America

The Captain America Heroes car is called the Hot Bird. It was based on a classic American sports car called the Pontiac Firebird. The car is red, white, and blue. "Captain America" is written on the side.

The Hot Wheels Spider-Man monster truck is red with a spider on top.

Hot Wheels has partnered with Marvel Comics several times since the 1970s.

The Captain America Heroes car was released in 1979.

DC Comics

In 1970, DC Comics created a *Hot Wheels* comics series. The series lasted for only six issues. Later, Hot Wheels made cars based on famous DC Comics superheroes and villains.

The *Hot Wheels* comics series lasted from 1970 to 1971.

A new Batmobile with blue rims was released in 2024.

The Batmobile

The superhero Batman has a famous car called the Batmobile. The Batmobile has changed its look across Batman comics, TV shows, and movies. Hot Wheels has made more than 20 versions of the superhero's car. The first Hot Wheels Batmobiles came out in 2004. Another was based on the Batmobile from the 1989 film *Batman*.

Hot Wheels has released more than a dozen versions of the *Millennium Falcon* starship.

Hot Wheels Lightsaber

Star Wars characters fight with swords called lightsabers. In 2014, Hot Wheels released a car based on the Star Wars villain Darth Vader. The car came inside a case that looked like Darth Vader's lightsaber.

Star Wars Hot Wheels

In 2014, Hot Wheels released a line of Hot Wheels Star Wars cars. These cars were inspired by Star Wars characters. A year later, Hot Wheels released a line of Star Wars starships.

Carships

In 2016, Hot Wheels released a line of Star Wars Carships. Like the 2015 line, these Hot Wheels were based on Star Wars starships. However, these Hot Wheels have wheels and are shaped like cars. Hot Wheels also released playsets for the Carships.

The Millennium Falcon was one of six Carship designs released in 2016.

The 2016 Super Mario cars featured six different characters.

Super Mario

Some Hot Wheels are based on video game characters. In 2016, Hot Wheels released a series of cars based on Super Mario characters. The set included cars designed to look like Mario, Luigi, Princess Peach, and Bowser.

Minecraft

Minecraft is a popular video game. In the game, players mine blocks to build things, including houses and machines. In 2017, Hot Wheels released Minecraft character cars. The cars look like characters from the video game.

Most of the 2017 Minecraft cars look like enemies from the video game.

Disney Hot Wheels

Hot Wheels has partnered with Disney several times to make character cars. Some of the cars are based on Mickey Mouse and his friends. Others are based on characters from Disney movies such as *Finding Nemo* and *Mulan*.

Hot Wheels has released more than 50 Disney character cars.

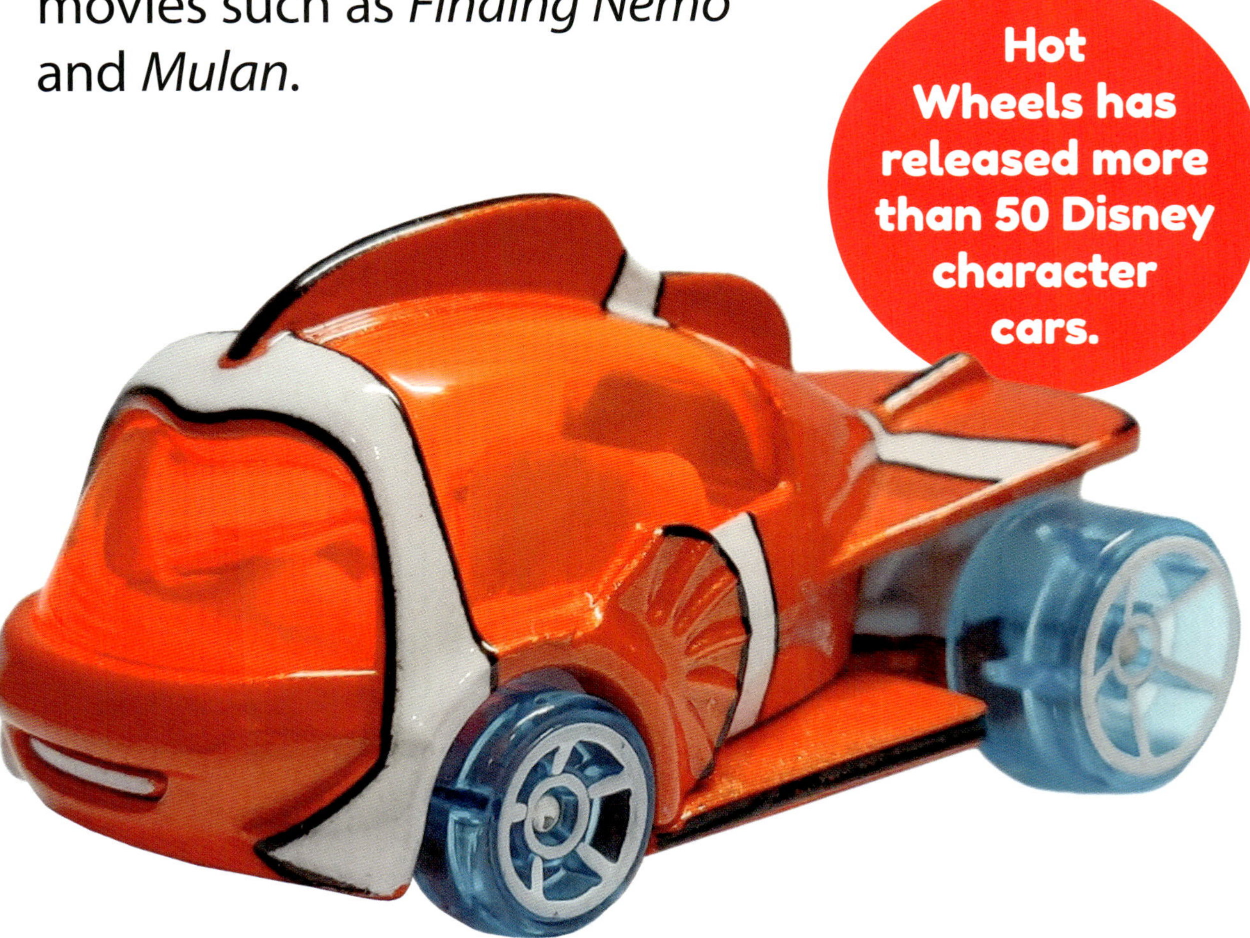

The
Winnie the Pooh
Hot Wheels was
designed by
Bryan Benedict.

Winnie the Pooh

The Winnie the Pooh Hot Wheels came out in 2018. The toy is shaped like a cement truck. These trucks have spinning barrels in the back where concrete is stored. The barrel on the Winnie the Pooh vehicle looks like the character's famous honey pot.

The first Jurassic World character cars were released in 2018.

Jurassic World

Hot Wheels created character cars based on a film called *Jurassic World*. The movie is about dinosaurs brought back to life in the present day. The character cars have dinosaur-inspired shapes and decals. There are also Hot Wheels based on the vehicles Jurassic World characters drive.

T-Rex Chomp Down

The T-Rex Chomp Down playset has a toy T-Rex in the middle of the set's track. Cars must race through its moving jaws.

Sanrio

In 2021, Hot Wheels partnered with Sanrio. Sanrio is a Japanese company that designs cute characters. Hot Wheels made cars based on several of the company's characters. One of the cars was based on Sanrio's famous Hello Kitty.

The Hello Kitty Hot Wheels was designed by Lindsey Lee.

Hot Wheels for Sale

Hot Wheels releases hundreds of new designs each year. New releases come out about every three weeks. The company has an online launch calendar. Fans can see when new Hot Wheels will be for sale.

Hot Wheels have cost about one dollar for the last 50 years.

If every Hot Wheels ever made was placed in a line, it would circle Earth four times.

Where to Buy Hot Wheels

Many stores sell Hot Wheels. Major retail stores carry them. So do big pharmacy chains. Cars are also sold online. Different stores often have different toys for sale.

Foreign Market Hot Wheels

Some Hot Wheels are only sold outside the United States. For example, some versions of the Dodge Rampage were sold only in Mexico.

Roughly 50 new mainline Hot Wheels designs are released every year.

Hot Wheels Basics

The regular Hot Wheels found in stores are part of the Hot Wheels Basics collection. This line is also called the Hot Wheels Mainline collection. These cars usually cost about one dollar. Sometimes these Hot Wheels are new designs. Sometimes they are older models with new paint and graphics.

FUN FACT!

Sometimes Hot Wheels are sold in packs of 20 for less than $20.

Blister Packs

Mainline Hot Wheels often come boxed in cardboard. A clear window lets buyers get a close look at the car inside. This kind of packaging is called a blister pack.

Some collectors leave their cars unopened to keep them in perfect condition.

The Porsche 935 is a Super Treasure Hunt Hot Wheels.

Treasure Hunts and Super Treasure Hunts

Treasure Hunts are rare Hot Wheels. These cars have special symbols on them. In a package of 72 Hot Wheels, one will be a Treasure Hunt. There are also Super Treasure Hunts. These Hot Wheels are even rarer.

Themed Assortments

Not all Hot Wheels sell for just one dollar. There are special toys that are more expensive. These are Themed Assortments. They are also called Silver Label Hot Wheels. They have a silver symbol. These Hot Wheels have higher-quality paint and designs.

In 2024, Hot Wheels released a Themed Assortment line of Porsche cars.

Hot Wagons

The Hot Wagons were a 2024 Hot Wheels Themed Assortment. There are five different cars in the set. Some are classic station wagons. Each is stamped with detailed graphics, including license plates, headlights, and taillights.

The Volvo 850 Estate was part of the 2024 Hot Wagons series.

Hot Wheels Premium

Hot Wheels Premium cars are also more expensive than regular Hot Wheels. These toys are generally made for adults who collect Hot Wheels. Premium cars have rubber wheels. They also have very detailed graphics.

Red Line Club

Red Line Club Hot Wheels are the highest-quality Hot Wheels. These Hot Wheels can be bought only by members of the Red Line Club. The cars cost about $25 to $40. They have the fanciest designs and features.

The Kawa-Bug-A was released exclusively for Red Line Club members.

Hot Wheels by the Numbers

Hot Wheels is one of the most beloved toy brands in the world.

130
new cars per year

20,000+
different cars

150
countries where Hot Wheels are sold

$1 billion+
in revenue per year

Joining the Red Line Club

It costs $9.99 per year to join the Red Line Club. Members get special benefits. They can buy some cars before other people. They also get updates about Hot Wheels news. They can chat online with other members.

Mattel estimates that there are 15 million Hot Wheels collectors.

What Makes a Hot Wheels Collectible?

Some people collect Hot Wheels. There are thousands of different toys to collect. Collectors usually like rare Hot Wheels best. These may be cars that have unusual colors. Display and sample toys are also rare. These Hot Wheels were not made to be sold.

Hot Wheels Collectors

Hot Wheels collectors can search for toys in many places. They may shop at big stores. They may buy old Hot Wheels on shopping websites. They may buy from other collectors online or in person.

Redline Shop

The Redline Shop is an online store. People can visit it to buy parts to fix their Hot Wheels.

Some stores have entire sections devoted to Hot Wheels.

Rare Hot Wheels Colors

Many Hot Wheels are made in several colors. The rarest colors are the most collectible. For example, the Rodger Dodger is a common early Hot Wheels car. Some were painted white on the inside. Today, these Rodger Dodgers are very valuable.

The original Rodger Dodger comes in plum, blue, and gold.

The 1968 White Custom Camaro

The 1968 White Custom Camaro is one of the most prized Hot Wheels. It was a prototype of the original Hot Wheels car. A prototype is an early version of a product. The White Custom Camaro may be the first Hot Wheels ever made. Today, it could be worth $100,000.

Cars with errors are also known as defects.

Errors

Some Hot Wheels are made with errors. These cars are very rare. This makes them expensive. Collectors often search for these Hot Wheels.

1969 Cheetah Base with Python Body

In 1969, Hot Wheels made a hot rod originally called the Cheetah. Partway through the design process, the car was renamed the Python. But a few of the cars were made with the name Cheetah on the base. These cars are very expensive now.

While Pythons were released in multiple colors, only red Pythons have been found with Cheetah bases.

Rare Hot Wheels

Hot Wheels does not tell people how many it makes of each toy. It can be hard to know which Hot Wheels are rarest. But some Hot Wheels, such as those for Red Line Club members, come in smaller numbers. These limited editions can be collectible.

While the exact number of Red Line Club cars made is unknown, it is estimated that 25,000 to 35,000 copies of each car are produced.

ZAMAC stands for zinc, aluminum, magnesium, and copper.

Exclusive ZAMAC Cars

Hot Wheels made special cars for the twelfth annual Hot Wheels Collectors Convention. These cars are called ZAMAC cars. ZAMAC is the name of the metal alloy that Mattel uses to make Hot Wheels. The ZAMAC cars were unpainted. Mattel made only 500 of each kind.

The Volkswagen Beach Bomb was designed by Ira Gilford.

The Pink Volkswagen Beach Bomb

The pink Volkswagen Beach Bomb was made in 1969. Prototypes of the toy van had surfboards in the back. This rear-loading design made the car unsteady. The Beach Bomb was redesigned with the surfboards on the sides of the car. But a few of the original cars found their way to the public. These cars are incredibly rare.

The Beach Bomb Today

Today, the pink rear-loading Beach Bomb is the world's most expensive Hot Wheels. It sells for $175,000. There are only two known pink rear-loading Beach Bombs in existence.

Collector Bruce Pascal owns more than 7,000 Hot Wheels, including a pink Beach Bomb.

Most Expensive Hot Wheels

The rarest Hot Wheels cost thousands of dollars.

$25,000

1968 Over Chrome Custom Camaro

$40,000

1968 Over Chrome Custom Mustang

$175,000

1969 Pink Rear-Loading Beach Bomb

Hot Wheels Tracks

Hot Wheels racers have many different tracks to choose from. There are tracks with loops and jumps. Some are motorized. These tracks make cars faster as they travel along the track.

Like character cars, some tracks are built with specific themes.

Track builders and expansion packs can be bought online or at big retail stores.

Track Builders and Expansion Packs

Some people like to customize their car tracks. Track builders and expansion packs let buyers do that. Track builders come with track pieces and connectors. People can decide on the shape and length of their homemade tracks.

FUN FACT!

The longest Hot Wheels track was more than 2,460 feet (750 m) long.

Glass cases can protect special Hot Wheels.

Hot Wheels Parking and Storage

People need somewhere to store their model cars. Hot Wheels sells parking garages for storing toy cars. Hot Wheels cases are also available.

Hot Wheels City

Hot Wheels City is a line of related toys. The city features racing tracks and car washes. There are also restaurants and garages. People can mix and match these toys.

Hot Wheels City sets are designed for kids aged three through eight, but anyone can play with them.

Hot Wheels Racing Kits

Hot Wheels Racing Kits were released in 2011. Each kit comes with two Hot Wheels vehicles and accessories. One kit comes with a truck and a snowmobile. The kit also includes toy snow, wood, and a plastic tree. Other sets come with roadblocks and cones.

Snow Race was one of the 2011 Hot Wheels Racing Kits.

The Ready-to-Race Night Shifter comes with 29 accessories for people to add to the car.

Putting Cars Together

Some people want to put their cars together. The Ready-to-Race kit lets them do that. These kits come with many car parts and toy tools. Buyers can put the cars together themselves.

Hot Wheels clothing is sold online and in stores.

Clothing

Mattel sells Hot Wheels clothing. There are many different Hot Wheels shirts. Some have the Hot Wheels logo. Others have pictures of certain cars. There are Hot Wheels hats and sweatshirts too.

Lunch Boxes

Mattel also offers Hot Wheels lunch boxes. These come in metal and soft options. The company sells matching Hot Wheels water bottles too.

The Hot Wheels Twin Mill lunch box came out in 1998.

Full-Size Vehicles

The Twin Mill was the first Hot Wheels to become a full-size car. A life-size Twin Mill was made in 2001. In 2003, Hot Wheels unveiled a life-size version of the Deora. Later, the company made a Pontiac GTO with special Hot Wheels decorations.

The life-size Twin Mill is a fully functioning car.

Hot Wheels bikes are generally designed for kids.

Bikes and Scooters

Mattel sells Hot Wheels bicycles. These bikes have the Hot Wheels logo. There are Hot Wheels scooters as well.

FUN FACT!

Hot Wheels sells finger skateboards.

Since its release in 1990, more than 40 versions of the Propper Chopper have been created.

Blimps and Helicopters

Not every Hot Wheels runs on the ground. Hot Wheels makes scale models of aircraft. The first Hot Wheels aircraft was a white news helicopter called the 1990 Propper Chopper. The next year, Hot Wheels sold its first blimp.

Airplanes

Hot Wheels made an airplane in 2000. This airplane was part of the McDonald's series.

These are Hot Wheels made for McDonald's kids' meals. There have been more Hot Wheels airplanes since then. Some have propellers that spin.

Blimps

A blimp is an aircraft held in the air by light gas. Hot Wheels blimps do not fly. But like many real blimps, Hot Wheels blimps have logos on their sides.

In 2024, Hot Wheels released an airplane that could be pulled by a car.

Hovercraft

Hot Wheels has made several hovercraft models. These are vehicles that float above the ground. Some of the hovercraft are original designs. Others are based on hovercraft from popular movies. There are two Hot Wheels hovercraft based on Star Wars vehicles. There is another hovercraft based on the car from the *Back to the Future* movies.

Both of the Hot Wheels Star Wars hovercraft are based on fictional vehicles called Landspeeders.

RRRumblers are kept stable with a clear frame attached to four wheels.

Motorcycles

In 1971, Larry Wood helped design the RRRumblers series. These are 1:32 scale motorcycles. Each has a human figure on top. RRRumblers can run on regular Hot Wheels tracks. Later, McDonald's offered a 1:64 Hot Wheels motorcycle.

The John Glenn Action Pack was released in 1998.

Spacecraft

Hot Wheels has models of fictional starships. The company also releases models of real spacecraft and rockets. The John Glenn Action Pack is based on the real astronaut's travels. It comes with models of the two spacecraft he flew in.

Space Rovers

Some vehicles explore other planets. These vehicles are called rovers. They collect information for scientists on Earth. In 1997, Hot Wheels sold the JPL Sojourner Mars Rover Action Pack. Each pack included a toy model of a Mars rover.

The National Aeronautics and Space Administration (NASA) partnered with Hot Wheels to design the JPL Sojourner Mars Rover Action Pack.

Boats

Hot Wheels has also made boats. The Hot Wheels H2GO Boat is a model speedboat. It has two engines on its back and wheels on its base. The speedboat was designed by Larry Wood.

The first H2GO Boat was released in 2008.

Submarines

In 1997, Hot Wheels made three submarines for its Undersea Adventure Action Pack. In 2016, Hot Wheels released a yellow submarine based on a song written by the British band the Beatles. It looks like the sub featured in the band's 1968 movie, *Yellow Submarine*.

The Commodore 64 cost $595 when it was released in 1982. That's nearly $2,000 in today's money.

Hot Wheels

The first Hot Wheels video game came out in 1984. It was called *Hot Wheels*. The game was released on the Commodore 64. This was an early home computer.

Playing the Game

In *Hot Wheels*, players choose one of six cars. They can change the car's color and parts. Players can then bring their cars to the car wash. They can fill cars with gas or change the oil.

FUN FACT!

In 2012 and 2013, Hot Wheels made video games that came free inside cereal boxes.

Old computer video games such as *Hot Wheels* were sold on devices called floppy disks.

Hot Wheels Thunder Roller

Hot Wheels Thunder Roller is a 1999 handheld racing video game. At the center of the device is a platform for a Hot Wheels car. Behind the platform is a screen. The screen shows a road with other cars. On either side of the device is half a steering wheel. Players tilt the wheel to avoid the other cars.

The *Hot Wheels Thunder Roller* game has multiple levels and tracks.

The Ford Stocker was designed by Larry Wood.

The Ford Stocker Car

The *Hot Wheels Thunder Roller* game came with a model Ford Stocker. It was based on a racing car. The model car moves as the game console tilts.

Video Games

There have been at least 40 different Hot Wheels video games. Some of the old games are playable online.

Hot Wheels is one of many companies that makes arcade racing games.

Hot Wheels Arcade Games

Arcades are places where people gather to play games. Hot Wheels arcade games let many players race at once. Each player gets a steering wheel. Players use the wheel to control a car on the screen.

Hot Wheels Pinball

Pinball is a popular type of arcade game. It dates back to the 1930s. Players use flippers to shoot a steel ball around a table covered with obstacles and bumpers. Hot Wheels pinball machines have Hot Wheels logos and graphics.

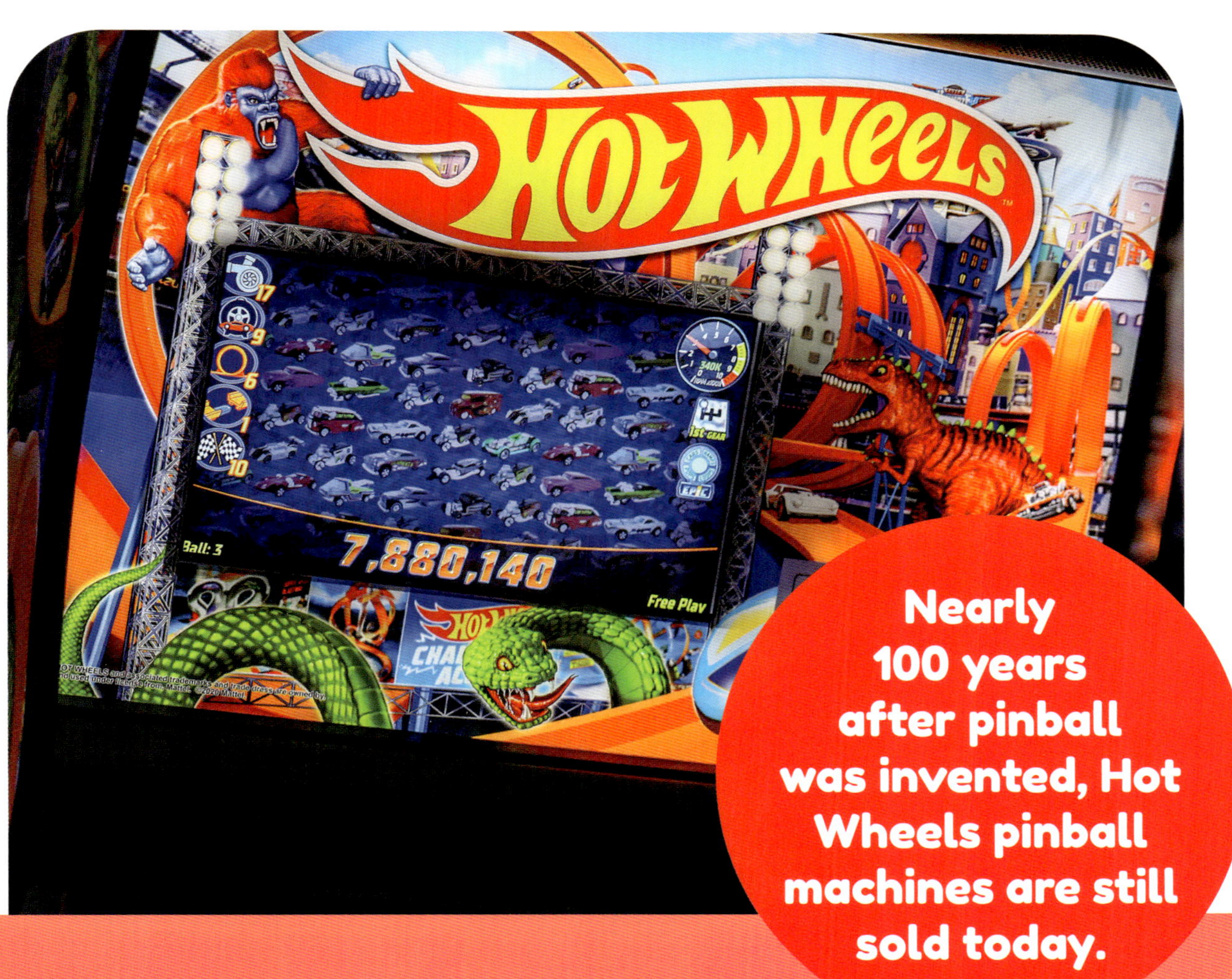

Nearly 100 years after pinball was invented, Hot Wheels pinball machines are still sold today.

Hot Wheels Unleashed

Hot Wheels Unleashed is a racing game. It was released for all major game consoles in 2021. In the game, players race through a room on mini Hot Wheels tracks.

***Hot Wheels Unleashed* offers expansion packs that include new cars and tracks.**

Hot Wheels Unleashed 2: Turbocharged can be played on the PlayStation, Nintendo Switch, Xbox, and computer.

Hot Wheels Unleashed 2: Turbocharged

Hot Wheels Unleashed 2: Turbocharged came out in 2023. It offers more than 130 different cars to choose from. Players can customize their cars and build racetracks. The game also includes a story mode where players can save a city.

***Hot Wheels* was targeted toward children.**

Hot Wheels on Television

The first Hot Wheels TV show came out in 1969. It was an animated Saturday morning show called *Hot Wheels*. The show is about two high school racing clubs. Each episode features a race.

Hot Wheels City

The *Hot Wheels City* TV series ran from 2018 to 2020. In the show, racers in Hot Wheels City fight thieves who are stealing car parts.

A Winning Design

At the end of the show, the winners of each episode competed again for the grand prize. The winning car design would become a Hot Wheels product. Arushi Garg was named the winner. She turned a Nissan into a symbol of bravery. The car had decals with messages such as "Never quit."

Arushi Garg's winning car was called the Rally Resilience.

Hot Wheels Let's Race

Hot Wheels Let's Race is an animated show. It came out in 2024. This show has six main characters. They are kids who are learning to be racers. Characters choose different cars for different races. Each car has different strengths.

***Hot Wheels Let's Race* features many real Hot Wheels, including the Roller Toaster.**

The Ultimate Garage playset can store more than 50 cars.

Ultimate Garage

In *Hot Wheels Let's Race*, the characters attend a racing camp at the Ultimate Garage. This multistory building has racetracks running through it. It is filled with Hot Wheels. Fans of the show can buy their own Ultimate Garage playset.

Team Hot Wheels performed at several events, including an extreme sports competition called the X Games.

Team Hot Wheels

From 2011 to 2017, four real car drivers were part of a group called Team Hot Wheels. They went by the nicknames Red Driver, Green Driver, Yellow Driver, and Blue Driver. The drivers performed stunts at racing events.

World-Record Jump

In 2011, Yellow Driver Tanner Foust set a world record for the longest ramp jump in a four-wheeled vehicle. He drove down a steep orange track. It looked like a giant Hot Wheels track. Foust drove his car into the air. It landed on a ramp 332 feet (101 m) away.

To get enough momentum to make his world-record jump, Tanner Foust drove down a ten-story-tall ramp.

Hot Wheels Monster Trucks Live

Hot Wheels Monster Trucks Live was created in 2018. During the show, drivers show off eight different monster trucks. They perform tricks and compete in five events, including a long jump contest.

Hot Wheels Legends

In 2018, Hot Wheels celebrated the brand's fiftieth anniversary with a tour called Hot Wheels Legends. Hot Wheels designers toured the country, holding car shows in 15 cities.

Each monster truck weighs 10,000 pounds (4,500 kg).

Attendants showed off their real cars, with the owner of the best car being declared the winner. The winner of each show competed for the grand prize. The grand champion had a Hot Wheels made based on the winning car.

The Hot Wheels Champion Experience was held in Tysons Corner, Virginia.

Hot Wheels Champion Experience

In 2023, the Hot Wheels Champion Experience opened in Virginia. The exhibit had a variety of activities. Visitors could draw cars on paper and place them in a scanner. A computer would then generate the design virtually. People could also race cars.

Hot Wheels Online

Hot Wheels fans can keep up with the brand on social media. There are also websites where collectors can show off their Hot Wheels. Other websites keep track of each new Hot Wheels.

Hot Wheels Museum

There is a Hot Wheels museum in Maryland. It is run by private collector Bruce Pascal.

Collectors can connect on social media and on Hot Wheels fan websites.

Hot Wheels Conventions

Fans can meet each other in person at Hot Wheels conventions. These are places to show off Hot Wheels collections. Conventions have vendors selling Hot Wheels products. Designers might come to sign autographs. People can share tips on collecting Hot Wheels.

Designers such as Jun Imai attend conventions to meet fans and teach people about Hot Wheels.

Hot Wheels Racing Meetups

Hot Wheels were made to race. And some people want to see how fast they can go. Fans bring their fastest Hot Wheels to racing meetups. They may bring customized cars as well. These meetups show the spirit of Hot Wheels. It's about going fast, being creative, and having fun.

GLOSSARY

alloy
A metal created by combining multiple types of metals.

assortment
A collection of different things.

automotive
Relating to vehicles.

chassis
The base of a vehicle.

convention
An event where people with a shared interest can meet.

conveyor belt
A moving surface that transports parts in factories.

customize
To take something and change parts of it.

decal
A sticker.

exhaust pipe
A pipe that gets rid of gases from a car's engine.

graphic
A picture or pattern.

logo
A symbol used to identify something from a certain brand.

mold
A hollow container used to make a consistent shape.

revenue
The amount of money made.

slogan
A short phrase that is used in advertising.

sports car
A low-built car designed to move fast.

voucher
A paper that can be exchanged for a good or service.

TO LEARN MORE

More Books to Read

Edwards, Sue Bradford. *Transformers*. Abdo, 2026.

Gale, Ryan. *Lego*. Abdo, 2026.

Hot Wheels: Ultimate Handbook. Mattel, 2025.

Online Resources

To learn more about Hot Wheels, please visit **abdobooklinks.com** or scan this QR code. These links are routinely monitored and updated to provide the most current information available.

PHOTO CREDITS